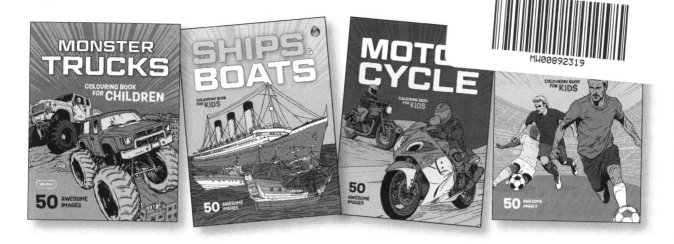

GET A FREE COLOURING BOOK

Dogs? Unicorns? Cars? Superheroes? Fashion?... The choice is yours!

Your feedback means an incredible amount to us. To say thanks for leaving us a review on Amazon we'd like to offer you a FREE COLOURING BOOK from our collection!

How to get your book

Simply leave an honest review of this colouring book on Amazon, then visit captaincolouringbook.com/claim to claim your free downloadable colouring book.

1 →

First, scan this to leave a review

2 →

Then scan this to claim your reward

© Copyright 2023 Captain Colouring Book
Cool Cars Colouring Book for Kids
50 Awesome Colouring Pages of Supercars, Hypercars, Race Cars and Classic Cars for Boys and Girls Aged 5 and up.
ISBN: 9798398132502

www.captaincolouringbook.com

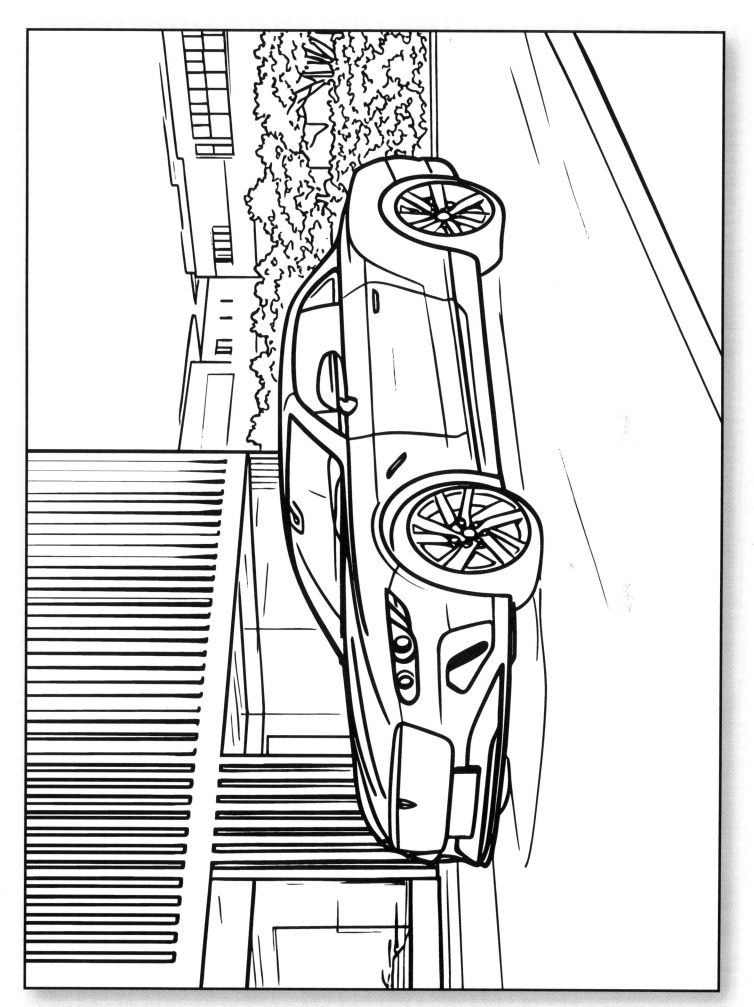

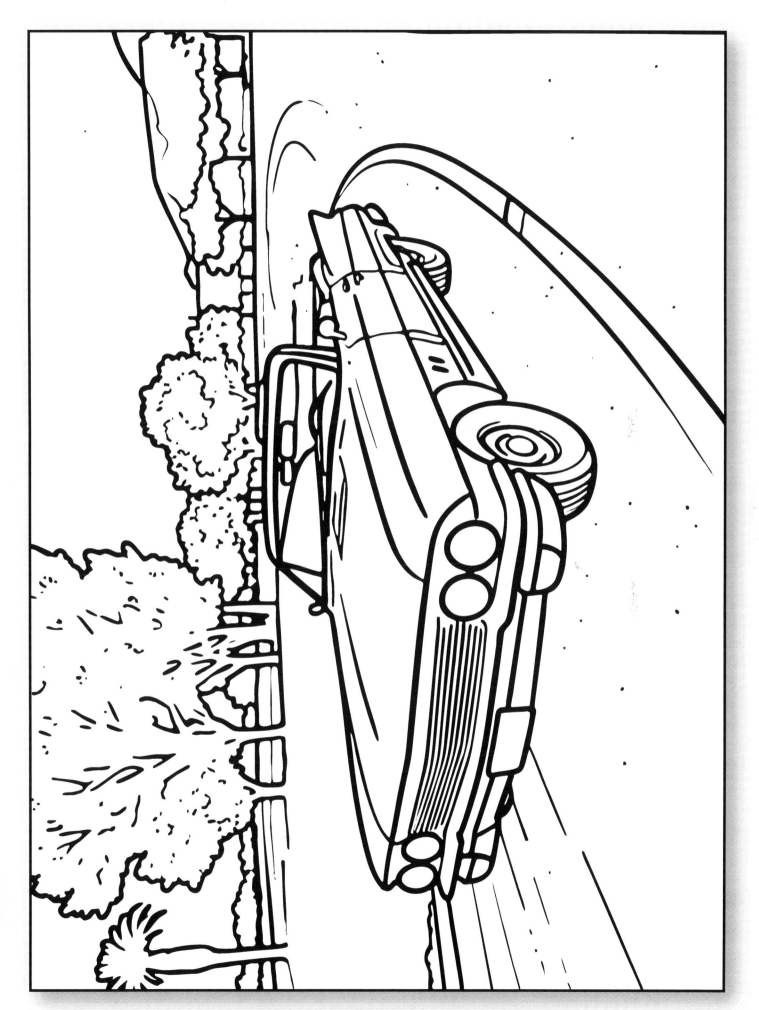

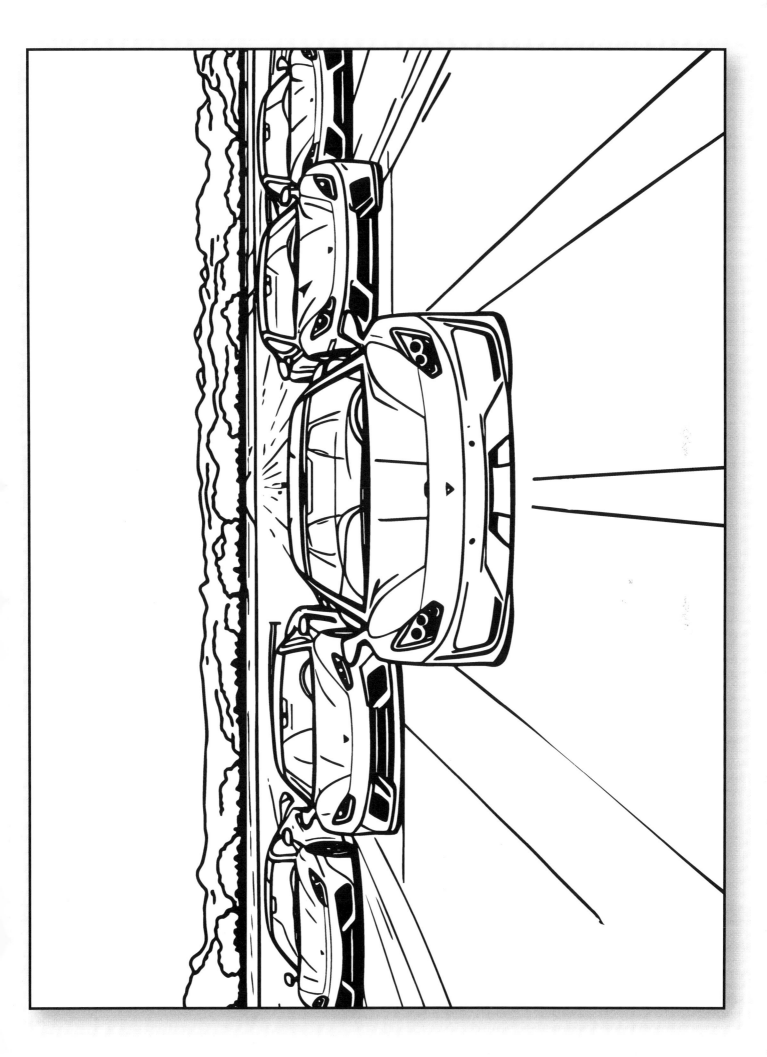

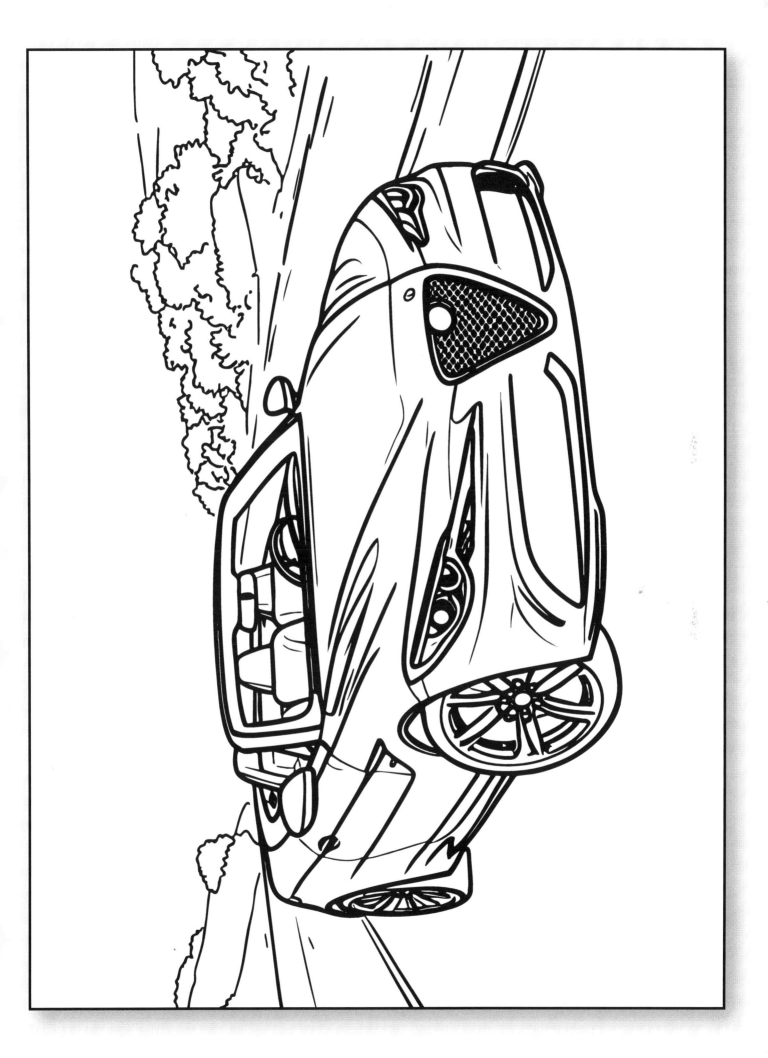

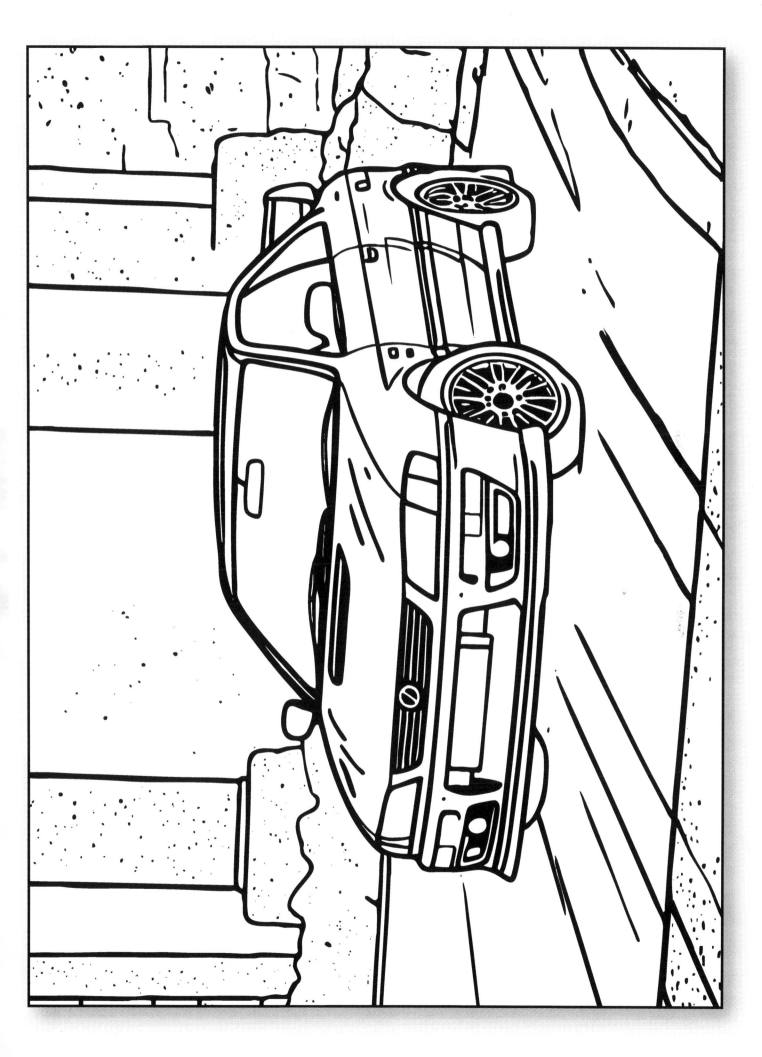

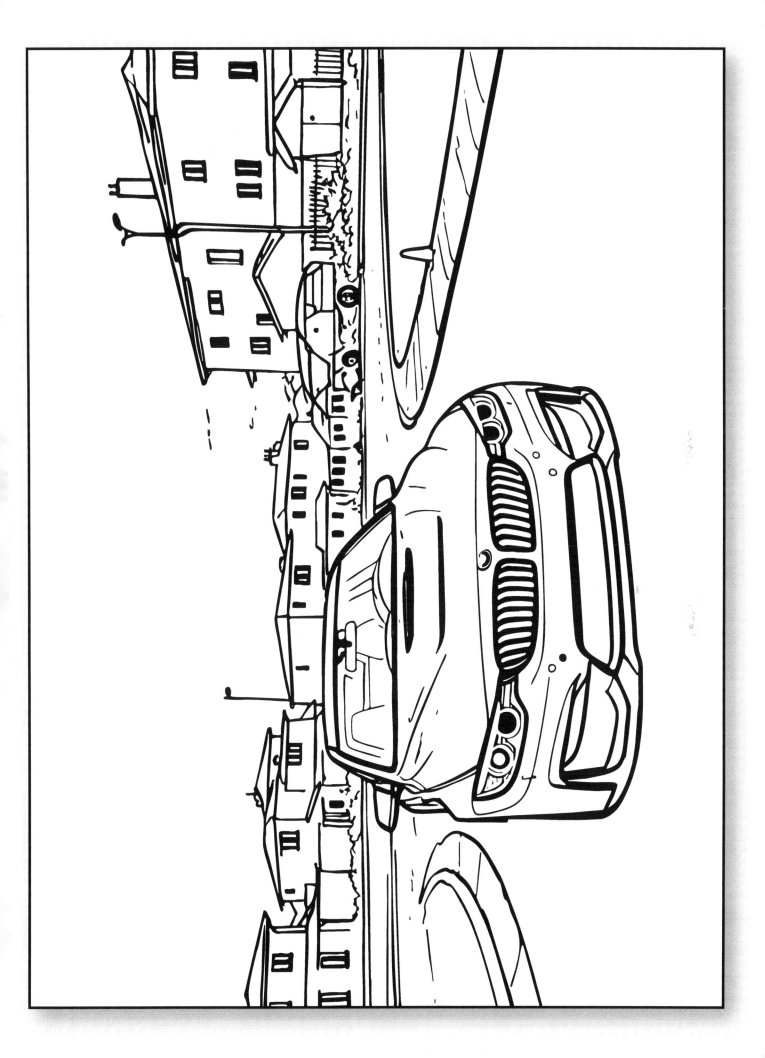

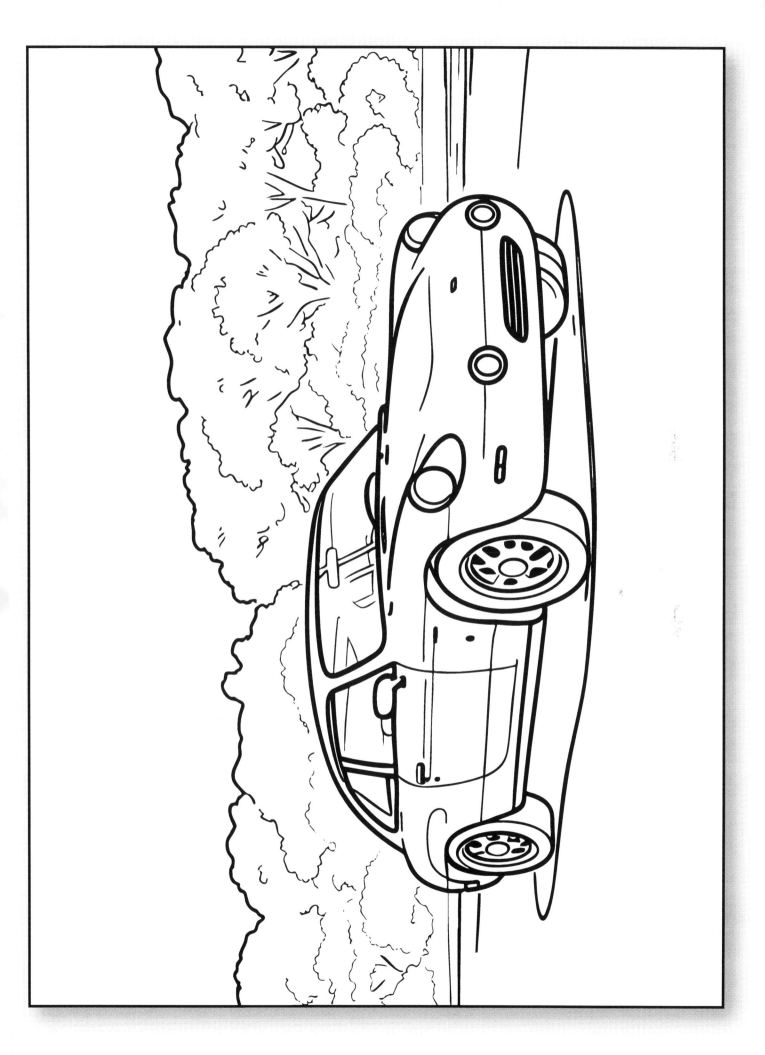

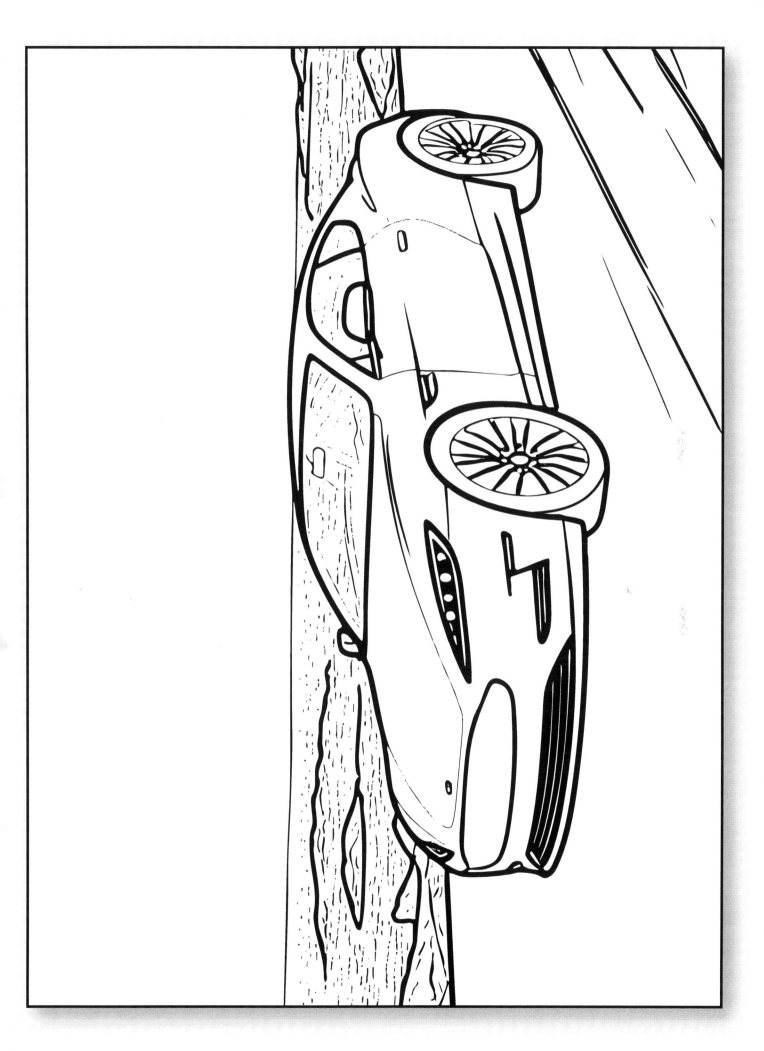

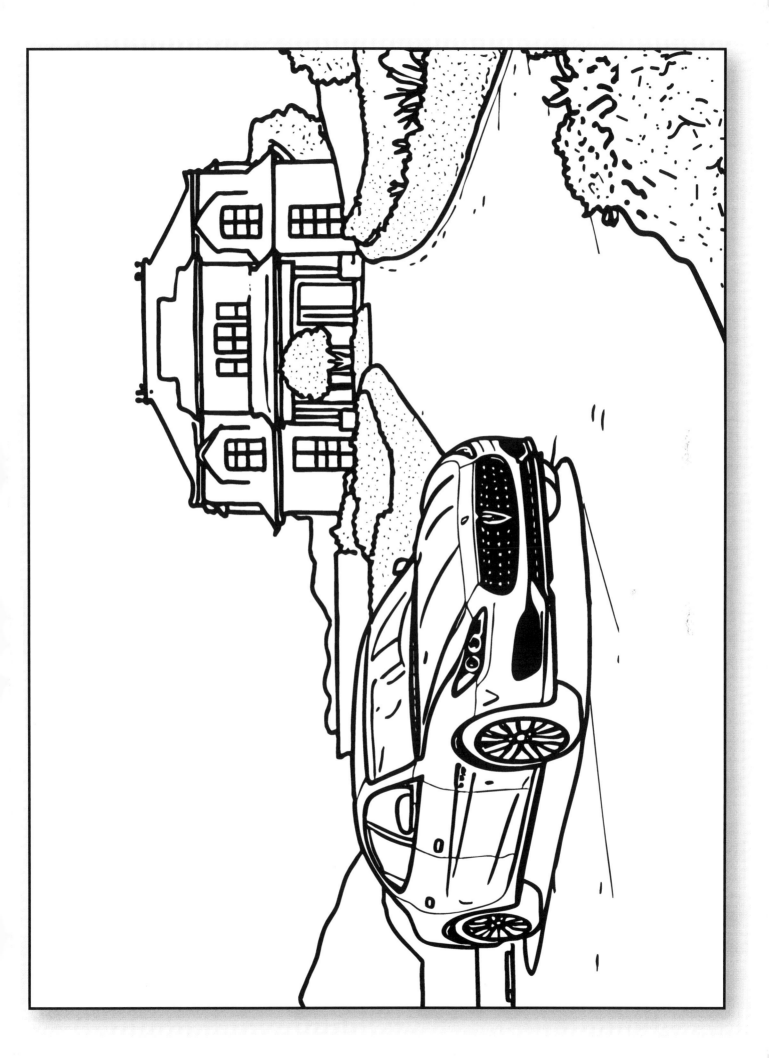

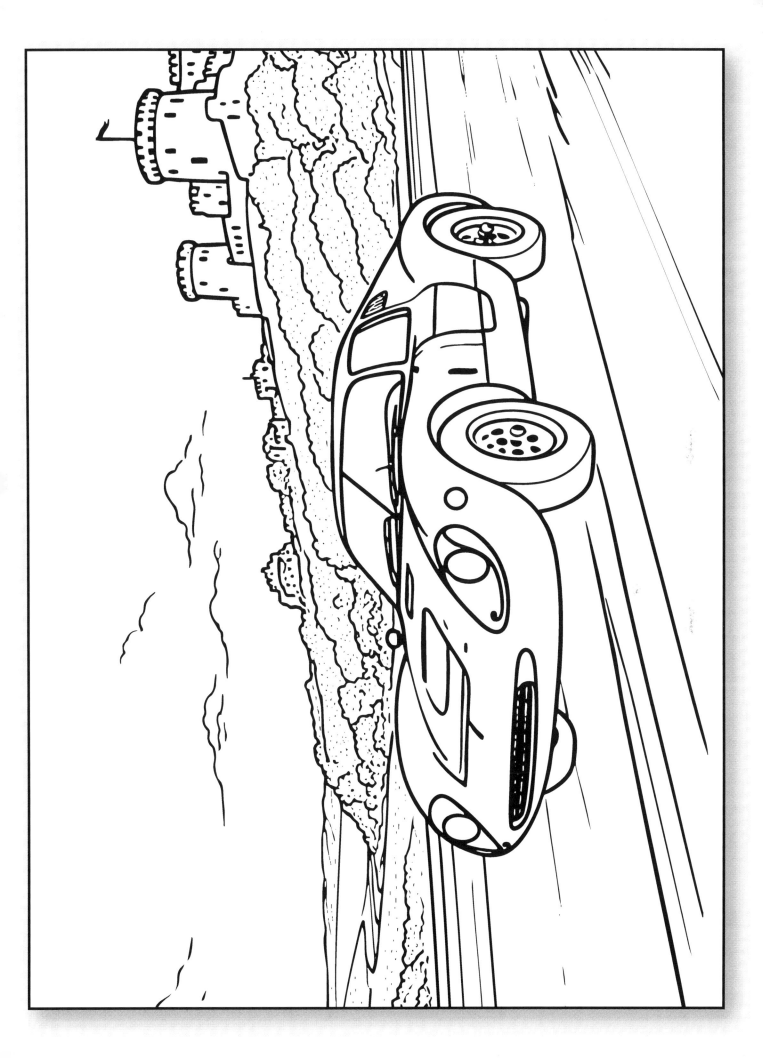

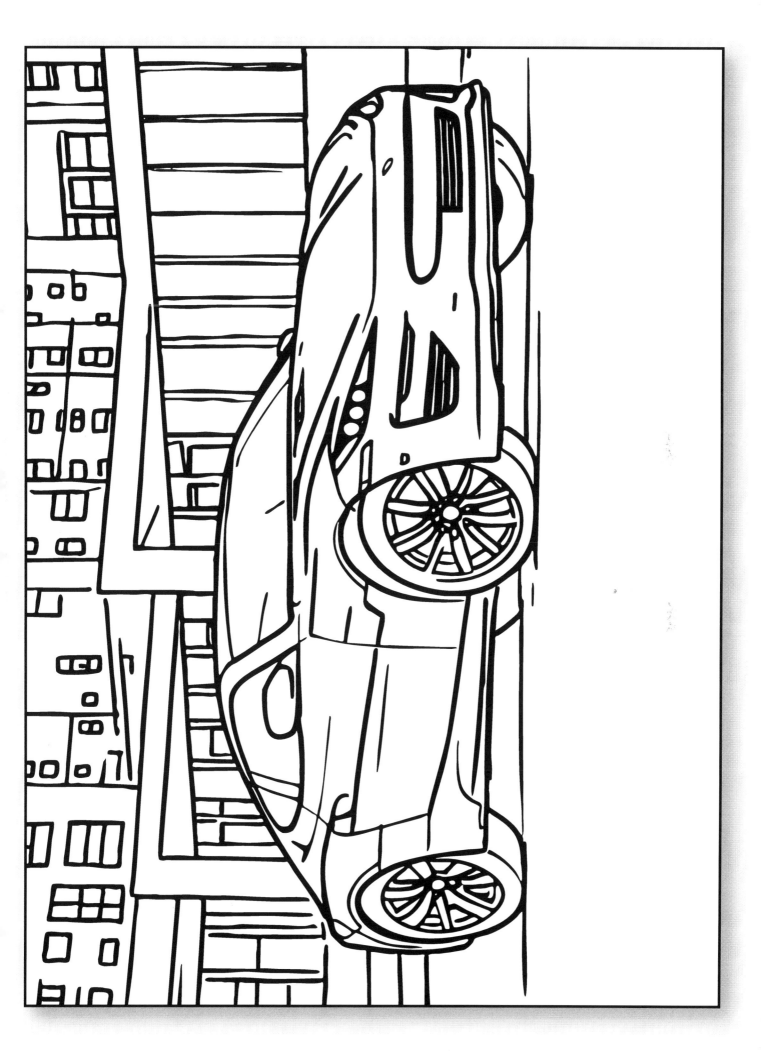

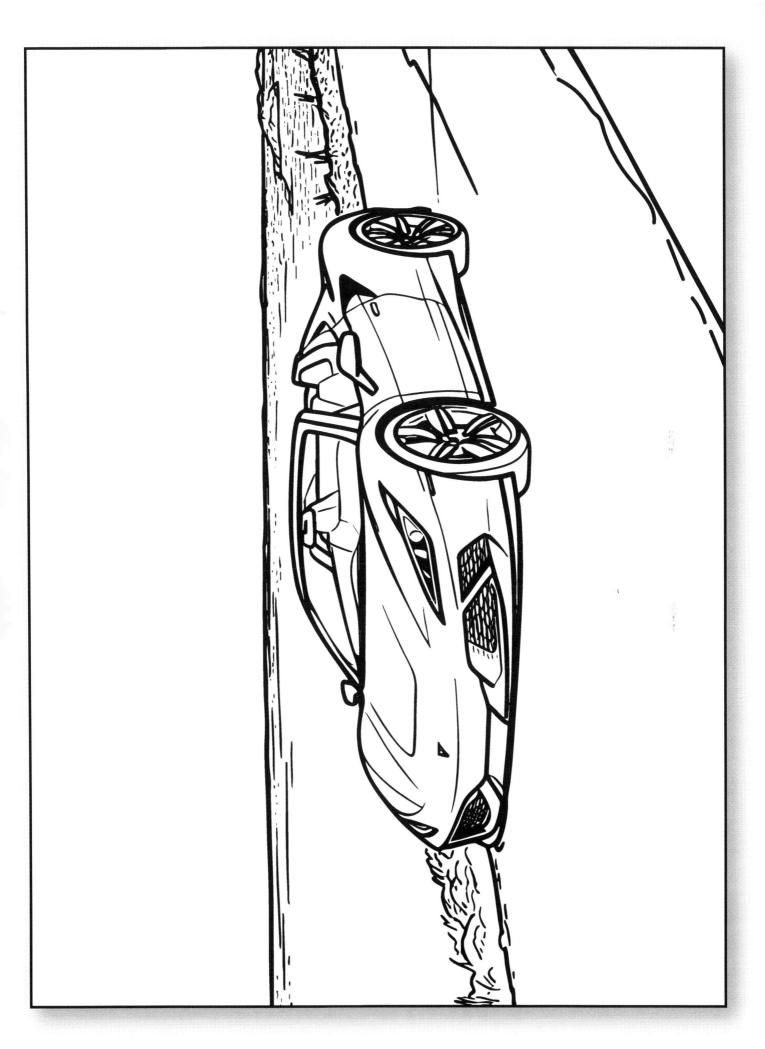

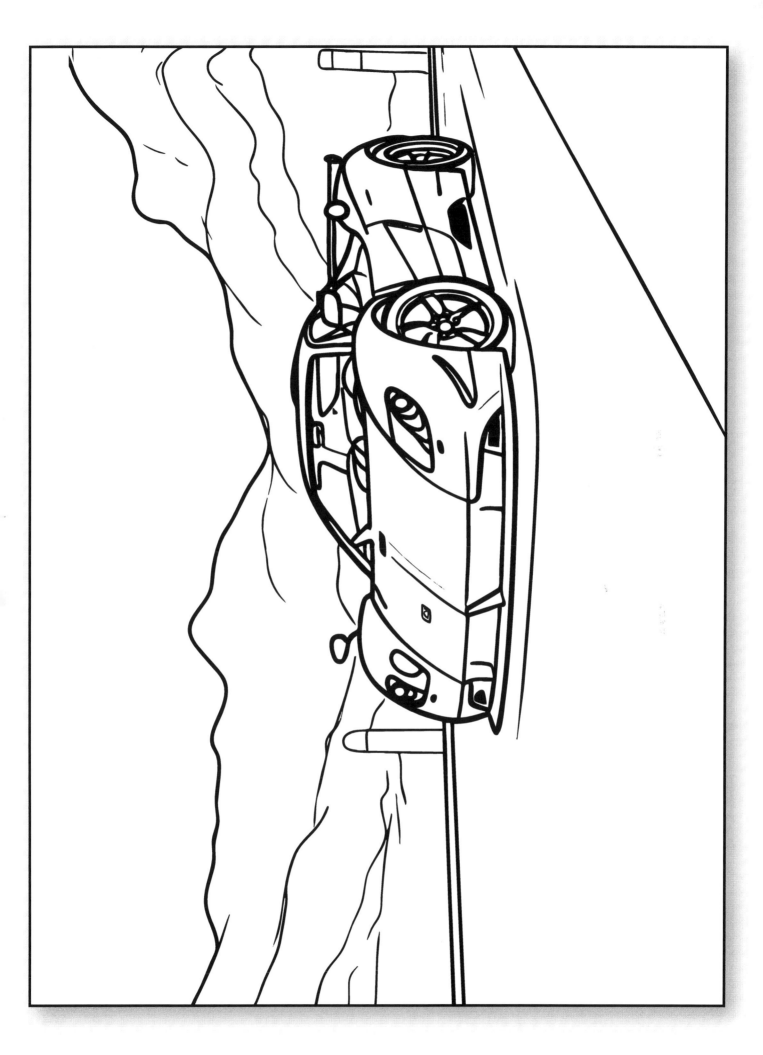

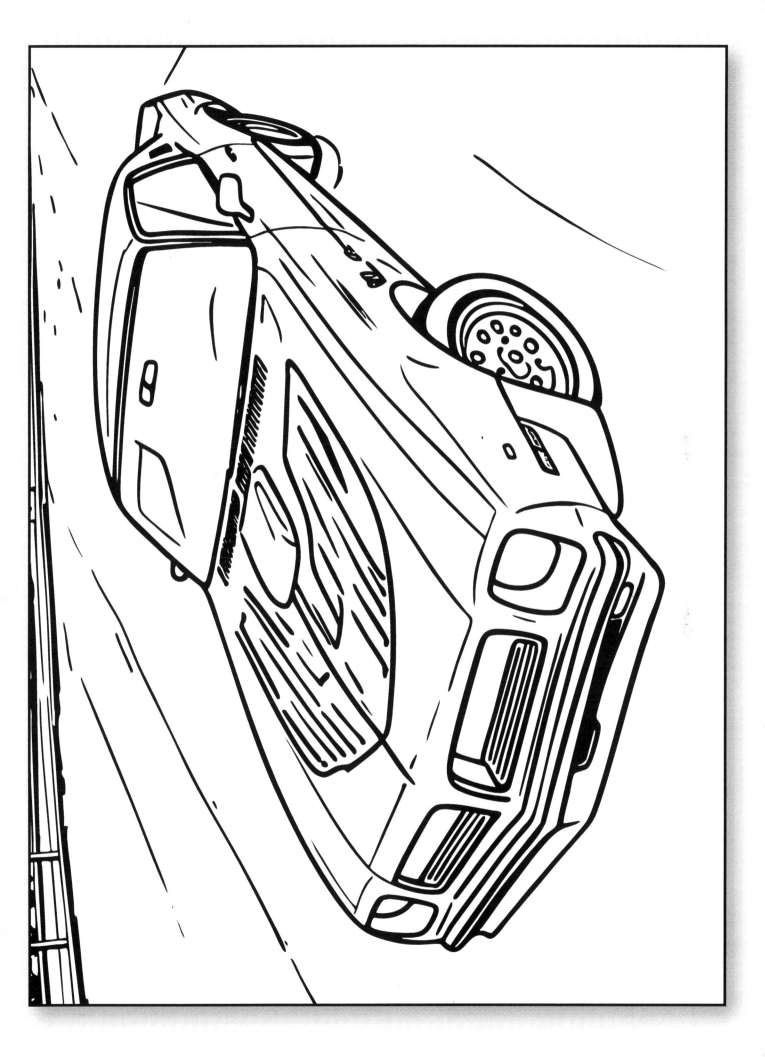

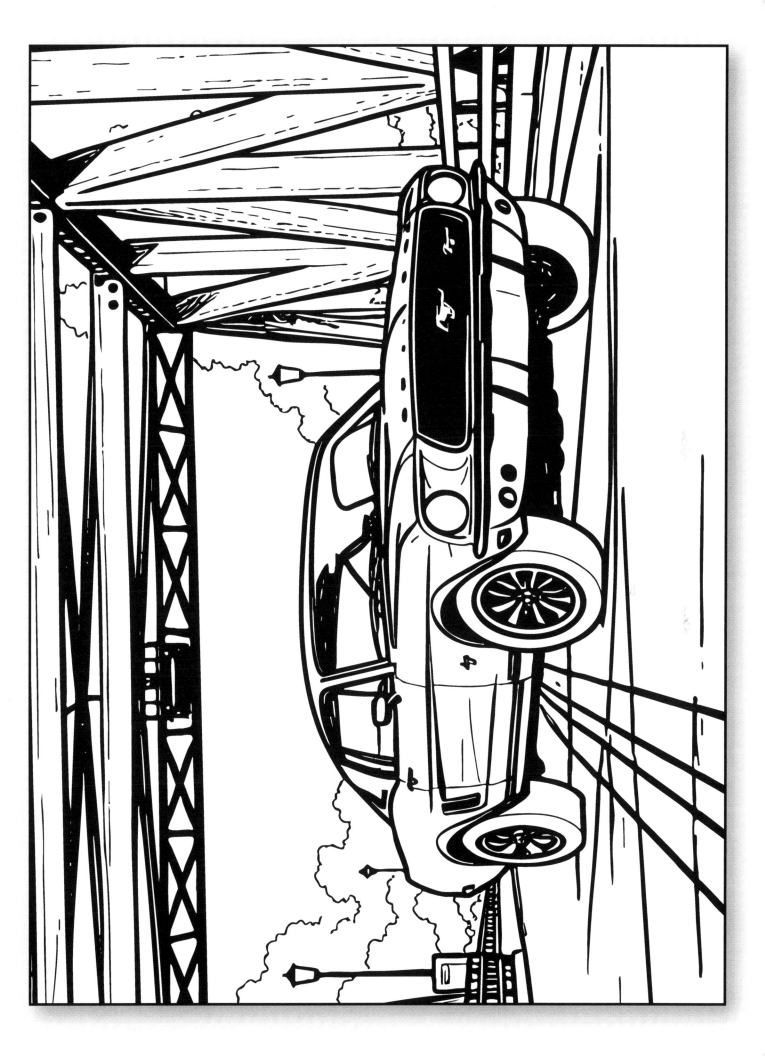

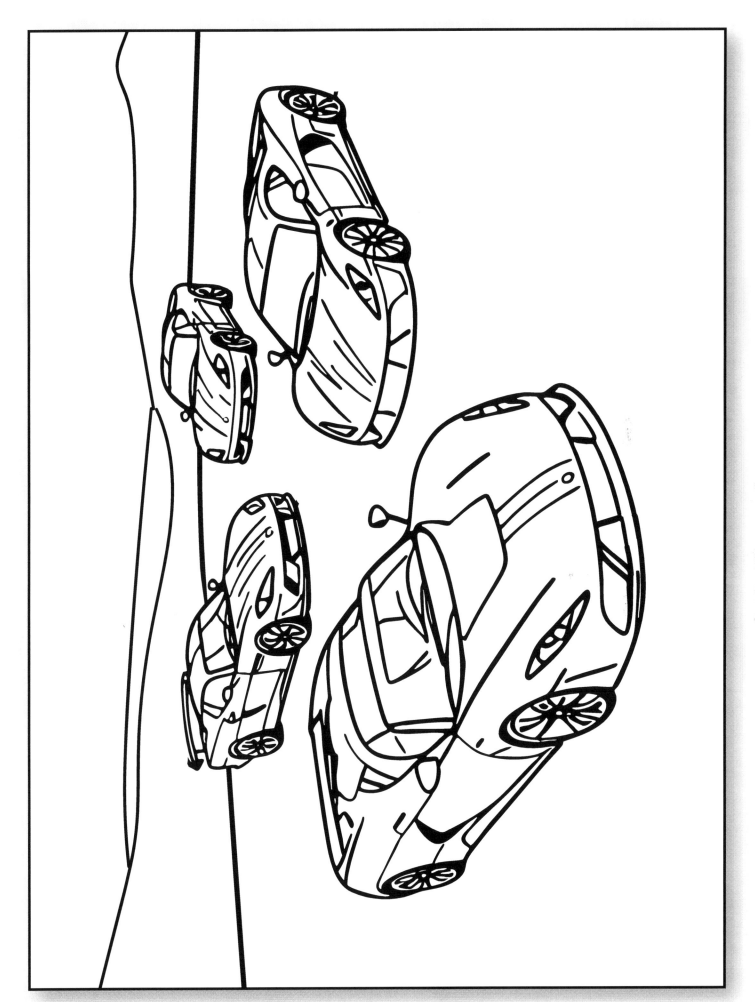

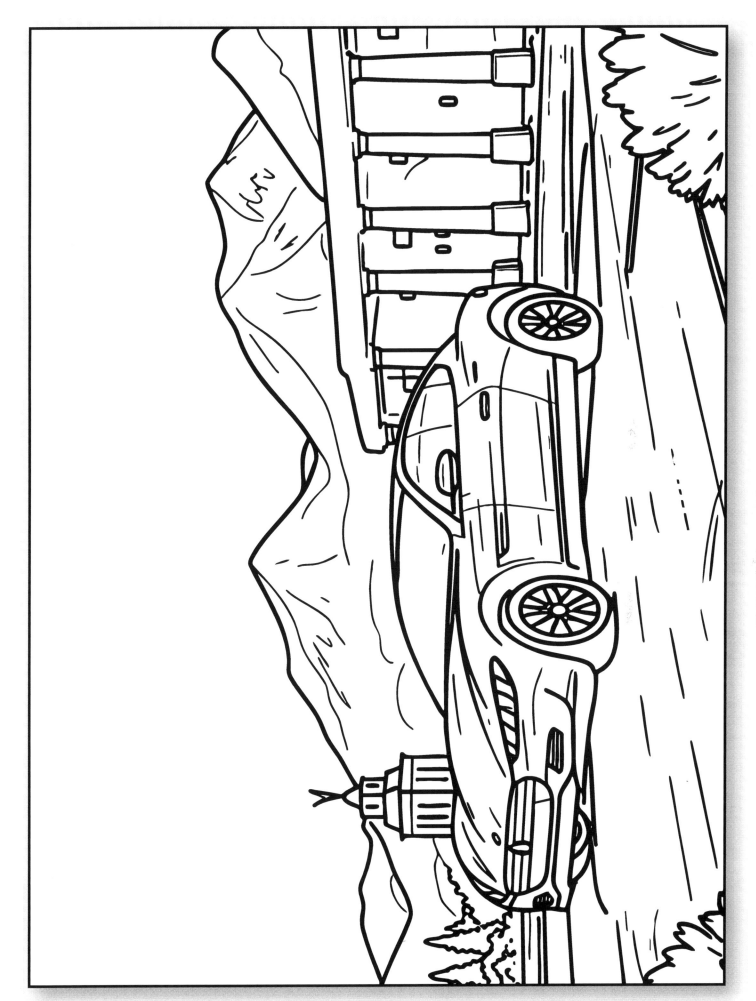

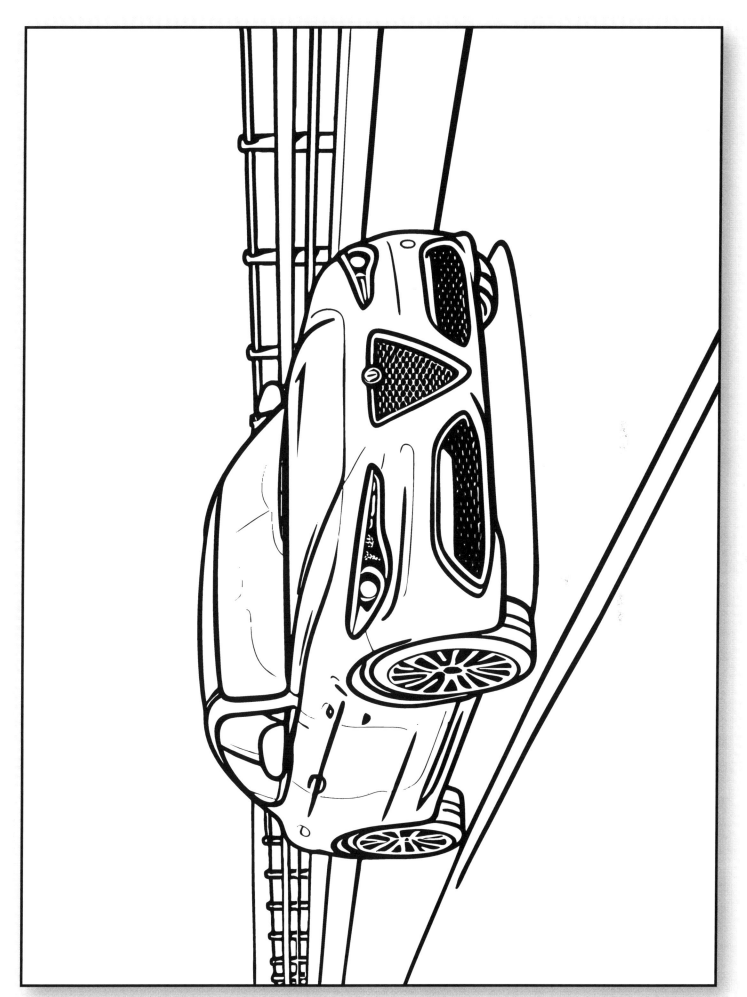

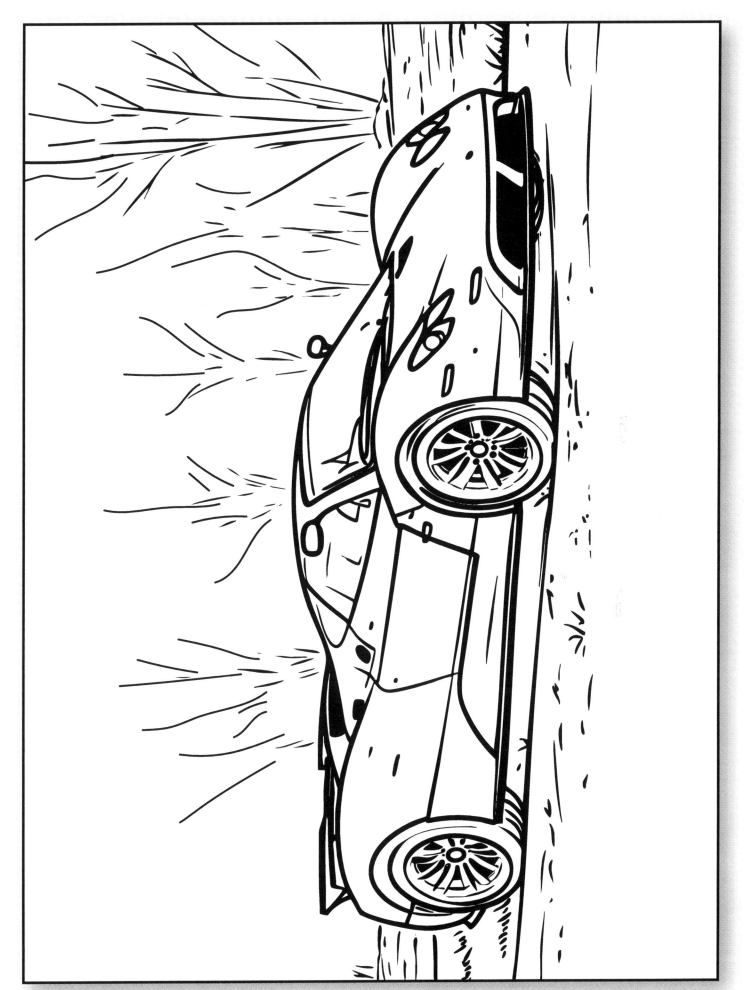

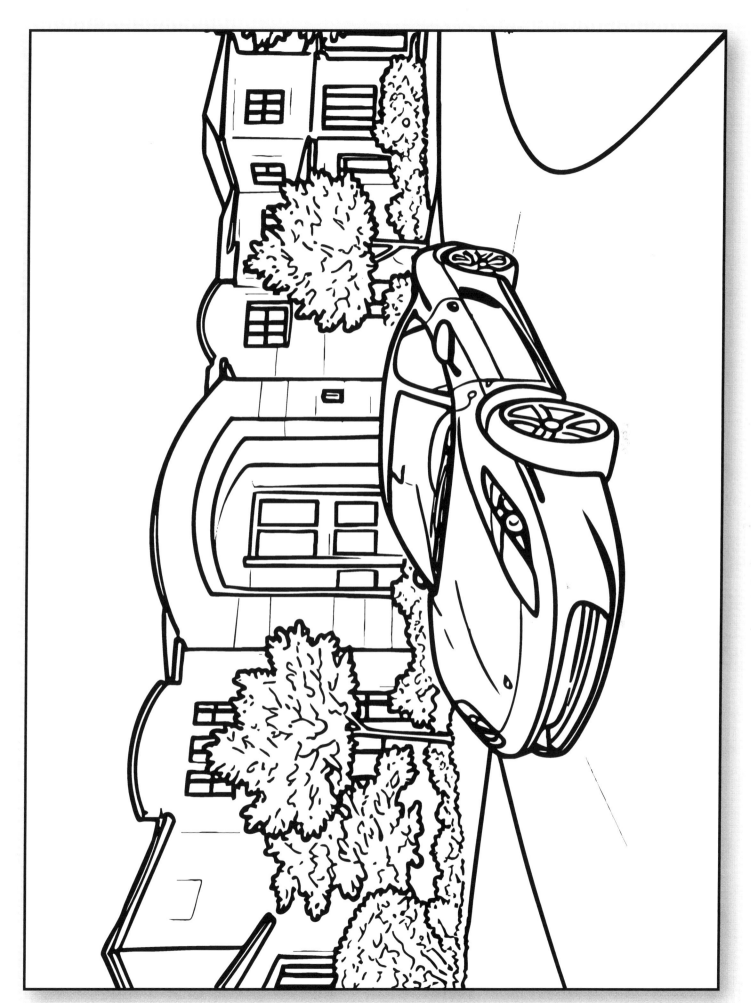

ALSO AVAILABLE FROM CAPTAIN COLOURING BOOK

Captain Colouring Book

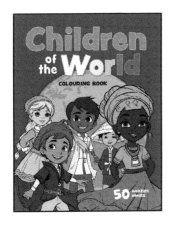  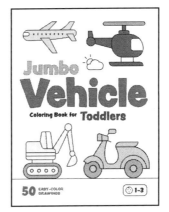 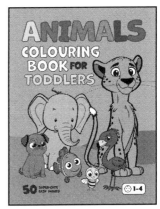

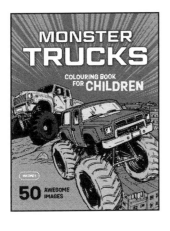  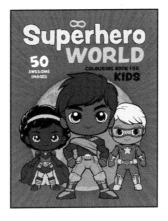 

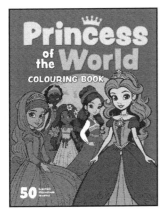  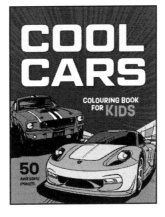 

Plus many more! To see the full collection visit
www.captaincolouringbook.com

Made in United States
Orlando, FL
05 December 2024

54955285R00059